Job Searching with Social Media

FOR DUMMIES

A Wiley Brand

Mini Edition

b

D1450300

FOR DUMMIES

A Wiley Brand

Job Searching with Social Media For Dummies®, Mini Edition

Published by: **John Wiley & Sons, Inc.,** 111 River Street, Hoboken, NJ 07030-5774, www.wiley.com

Copyright © 2014 by John Wiley & Sons, Inc., Hoboken, New Jersey

Published simultaneously in Canada

For general information on our other products and services, please contact our Customer Care Department within the U.S. at 877-762-2974, outside the U.S. at 317-572-3993, or fax 317-572-4002. For technical support, please visit www.wiley.com/techsupport.

Wiley publishes in a variety of print and electronic formats and by print-on-demand. Some material included with standard print versions of this book may not be included in e-books or in print-on-demand. If this book refers to media such as a CD or DVD that is not included in the version you purchased, you may download this material at http://booksupport.wiley.com. For more information about Wiley products, visit www.wiley.com.

ISBN 978-1-118-86148-6 (pbk); ISBN 978-1-118-86151-6 (ebk);
ISBN 978-1-118-86144-8 (ebk)

Manufactured in the United States of America

10 9 8 7 6 5 4 3 2 1

Table of Contents

Introduction

• •

In the modern job market, no tool is more capable of shortening your job search and helping you become successful in your career than *social media* — online networks that foster interaction with other people. Social media tools have become key resources for hiring managers who, on smaller budgets, turn to their network to fill positions. If you're ready to take your career to the next level, this book is your guide to using the online tools available to aid in both your job search and self-promotion.

About This Book

This book is your go-to reference for all kinds of tips and tricks that reveal how to use social media to find a job. Whether you're new to social media or are a seasoned social networking butterfly, you'll find information of value within this book.

Even if you think you know a lot about posting résumés online or using tools like LinkedIn, Twitter, and Facebook, I encourage you to give each chapter in this book a look. You may find new ideas or even old ideas used in new ways. These days, when you're searching for a job, any trick that separates you from the crowd is worth finding out about.

Icons Used in This Book

Keep your eyes peeled for the following icons, which I've scattered throughout the text to draw your attention to important paragraphs.

If you take nothing else away from this book, be sure to recall the information flagged with this icon.

This bull's-eye leads you to information I find to be particularly useful.

The information they contain is there to keep you from making a potentially career- or reputation-harming mistake.

Where to Go from Here

Chapter 1 gives you an overview of the social media tools available today. If you need help modernizing your résumé with social media in mind, jump to Chapter 2. Chapters 3, 4, and 5 get you started using LinkedIn, Twitter, and Facebook.

Of course, in this mini book, I can only cover the very basics. For much more help and advice, check out the latest version of *Job Searching with Social Media For Dummies*. Go to dummies.com or head to your favorite bookseller to pick up a copy.

Chapter 1

The Lowdown on Social Media for Job Hunters

. . . .

In This Chapter

▶ Realizing why you need to have an online presence when searching for a job

▶ Showing recruiters and hiring managers what makes you uniquely qualified

▶ Using social media sites to host your résumé and manage your online reputation

. . . .

Social media has become an important tool for job seekers due in part to the new ways people are finding out about (and getting fired from) jobs. As you may already know, most jobs come about through networking, not applying on job boards or aimlessly sending out résumés. Social media tools make networking much easier and much more powerful due to their interactive nature. Thus, when a job seeker really learns to use social networking well, his chances for finding opportunities multiply exponentially.

In this chapter, I help you grasp the bigger picture of why having more than a basic online presence is essential. I also help you figure out how to do all the prep work necessary for job searching with social media.

Why Your Online Presence Is Important

Information for just about everyone can be found online by someone who knows how to conduct the right search. That's right. Personal information such as your name, address, and phone number are on the Internet. But if you really want to use social media as a tool to land your dream job, then you need to be willing to expand your presence online beyond just the basics. I explain why in the sections that follow.

Whether or not you can do the job you're applying for will certainly help you pass screening and get your foot in the door. However, final decisions about your employment come down to your personality. Surveys have found over and over again that *fit* is the primary reason for hiring one person over another. And one of the best ways to prove how well you can fit in at one of your target companies is by using social media sites to reveal your personality. A printed-out résumé (or even one viewed on a computer screen) can only witness to your skills; a profile on a social media site can demonstrate your passion, your personality, and your uniqueness.

✔ **Recruiters will Google you.** Regardless of whether you search for your name online to see what comes up, you can bet that someone else will — namely the hiring managers at most (if not all!) of the companies you apply to. In fact, many recruiters I've interviewed have told me that conducting Internet searches (mostly through Google) on the people they're placing is part of their due diligence and responsibility. In other words, they wouldn't be doing their jobs if they *didn't* investigate your online presence.

✔ **Hiring managers are cheap.** Hiring managers' jobs are primarily not about hiring new employees; their day-to-day role usually has little to do with hiring because they're paid for their performance at other functions. They're going to rely on the cheapest and fastest ways of getting a stack of résumés, which often means leveraging their employees' referral network, LinkedIn, and maybe even Twitter. They want to get through the process of finding the right candidate as quickly as possible so they can focus on other priorities.

✔ **Generic résumé blasts don't work.** If all you're doing is sending your résumé out to numerous companies via job boards and hoping for a phone call, I'm not certain you'll make it past the screening process at most companies or organizations. Why? Because the company may be wading through hundreds of other generic-looking résumés. And when candidates send out general applications without researching the job, they can even get blacklisted.

Getting Ready to Start Your Search

Job seekers of earlier generations had one main tool at their disposal: the résumé. But thanks to the hundreds of social media sites out there, you have access to a lot more tools that can aid you in your job search — if you don't become distracted. If you've ever spent hours on Facebook by accident, checking out what your friends are up to, then you know just how easy it is to forget all about why you got online in the first place. Fortunately, you can keep yourself from becoming distracted (and, therefore, take full advantage of social media sites and make progress toward finding a job) by doing a little prep work before you begin your job search.

First, establish clear goals for yourself. Start with your end goal (getting a job interview), and then work your way backwards, step by step. Each step must be clear and simple to complete. By breaking down your goals into smaller chunks, you're less likely to feel overwhelmed. These smaller steps become the basis of how you spend your time, so every time you sit down to work, you know what to do.

It also helps to have some ideas for how you're going to manage your time. One way to go about that is by looking at your job search as a job in itself. Define the hours of the day you plan to work on finding a job and figure out how much time you're going to spend on certain tasks, such as profile writing, researching, or reaching out.

Naturally, you also need a way to keep all the information about your various contacts organized. After all, you're going to be meeting new people in person and adding them to your LinkedIn contact list, and then you're going to use Twitter and Facebook to discover what your network is up to.

Standing Out with a Personal Brand

Personal branding — the art of communicating what makes you unique — has been around for a long time. Everyone has a personal brand, even you, because everyone is unique. But not everyone is good at expressing this differentiation. Those people who are seemingly irreplaceable prosper in any economic situation.

To figure out your personal brand, you need to take a serious look at your core existence. Really strive to understand your values, passions, and strengths. In other words, figure out what makes you you.

After you're able to articulate what makes you unique, you can transform that knowledge into a value statement that expresses your worth and fit to prospective employers. By expertly communicating your value statement across several different mediums, you can grow your credibility and your brand influence.

Blogs make an excellent medium for communicating your value statement because they also allow you to share your knowledge and opinions about topics that matter to your particular field of interest. An added bonus of blogging? Employers who see you passionately turning out articles, videos, or slides in the area of your expertise will see that you're truly passionate about your work and have a depth of knowledge that may help their organization. Also, not many other candidates are brave enough to put themselves out there and share their voice.

A huge part of branding is making sure your brand is represented accurately and consistently at all times. You therefore need to manage your online reputation by taking charge of the results that come back when someone does an Internet search for your name.

Here are the basic steps for managing your online reputation:

1. **Assess your online appearance from the perspective of a hiring manager.**

   Try Googling yourself or searching for your name in a free background check website like www.pipl.com.

2. **Build up enough content over time so Google's search results fill up with more relevant content.**

3. **Monitor your reputation monthly.**

   If someone says something bad about you, you need to know about it right away. The only way to do that is by periodically searching for your name and seeing what pops up.

Putting Your Résumé Online

An online résumé can be searched and discovered by recruiters looking for talent, so having several of them increases your odds of being found. The beauty of online résumés is that you don't have to be a web designer to enjoy their benefits.

At the very least, you should have a LinkedIn profile and a video résumé. If you want to have more than just these two online résumés, good for you!

Writing an online résumé is very different than writing a résumé that you intend to print out and hand to someone. Don't think you can just copy and paste one into the other. (If you try that, your online presence can look stuffy, old fashioned, and hard to understand.)

LinkedIn (www.linkedin.com) happens to be the highest-leverage tool for professional networkers today — period. With it, you have access to more information about companies and people than previous generations ever did — even if they paid for it! Study after study has shown that LinkedIn is the primary resource for hiring managers and recruiters to fill positions. If you aren't using it daily, you're making a huge mistake.

To get the most benefit out of LinkedIn, don't just treat it as an online résumé. Instead, treat it as a professional networking tool. In fact, use LinkedIn as your networking hub. Sure, it may be easier to cruise job boards, but by regularly adding new people you meet to your network and getting so familiar with LinkedIn that you can use it in your sleep, you're going to have a better shot at finding a job at your target company.

Expanding Your Online Presence

 As your online presence grows, so do your chances of getting discovered by a recruiter and receiving an unsolicited call.

Getting yourself on Twitter and Facebook, if you aren't already, is worth your time. Twitter (www.twitter.com), which I cover in Chapter 4, is hands down one of the most active recruiting tools (aside from LinkedIn, which I cover in Chapter 3). Not a day goes by that some HR recruiter or hiring manager doesn't hit up Twitter searching for talent. As for Facebook (www.facebook.com), which I cover in Chapter 5, the best avenue into a target company is through your trusted friends and family. By building trust and making your intentions clear to your friends, Facebook will quickly become your most powerful (and secret) weapon for career advancement.

Conquering common objections to using social media in your career

What follows are some common objections that people pose to the idea of using social media in a career, and why those objections just don't pan out:

- ✔ **Social media is for kids on cellphones.** Au contraire! The fastest growing demographic on Facebook is 55 and older, and the average age of a Twitter user is 35. Also, all social media sites have desktop interfaces, so you can access them without using your cellphone.

- ✔ **I'm concerned about identity theft.** Honestly, you have more chances of getting your identity stolen from snail mail than from hacked social networks. Just be smart about the information you reveal. Remember: Keep the following to yourself at all times: your Social Security number, your mother's maiden name, and your birth date.

- ✔ **I don't have a lot of time, and I don't need another distraction.** Setting up your accounts on various social media sites may take some time, but from there on out, staying on top of social media shouldn't cost you much time.

Chapter 2

Updating Your Résumé for an Online Audience

. . . .

In This Chapter

▶ Fitting a traditional résumé into a modern job search

▶ Making an attractive résumé that's custom fit to you

▶ Using and writing recommendations

. . . .

*W*hen most people start a job search, they exclaim with some anticipation, "Now I have to update my résumé!" Although a traditional, hard-copy résumé *was* the pivotal part of a job search in the past, today a truly successful job seeker may never actually need one.

This chapter examines the way HR departments and hiring managers use résumés today. By understanding the function of a résumé, you can break free of the limitations it imposes on you. This chapter also shows you how to transform yesterday's paper résumé into a modern, web-based version with greater impact on your personal brand. Finally, you discover how obtaining and writing recommendations works in the social media world (goodbye writing your own long-winded letters; hello short and sweet recommender-generated content!).

Customizing Your Online Résumé

With social media, you have an opportunity to not only clarify whether you can do the job but also help a hiring manager determine your motivation level and whether you'd be a good fit for the company long before you reach the interview stage. In fact, if you've run your job search right by using the many social media tools available, you may hear a hiring manager say at the first interview, "I feel like I already know you."

When transferring your résumé to the web, the last thing you want to do is simply copy and paste your hard-copy résumé into an online format. If you do, you miss out on an opportunity to demonstrate the type of person you are and how motivated you are. Also, people read a computer screen differently than a piece of paper. Consequently, the way you write and format your online résumé should change accordingly. The sections that follow show you how to convert a traditional hard-copy résumé (see Figure 2-1) to one that shines online (see Figure 2-2).

Jane Doe

1234 SW 56th Place, Portland, OR 97223 · 503.222.2222 · hiremenow@hotmail.com

Professional Profile

Seasoned digital marketing strategist and director with deep knowledge of brand stewardship. 17 years experience blending customer insight, creativity, and technology to forge visionary brand experiences. Adept at bringing new brands to market, demonstrating thought leadership and enabling cross-functional collaboration. Consummate presentation skills.

Professional History

Independent Contractor, Portland, OR Present
SOCIAL MEDIA CONSULTANT
Focused on social media marketing for B2C and B2B brands. Expertise covers all facets of social media: strategic planning, content development, influencer relations, program management, analytics/optimization and operations.

Watz it Creative, Portland, OR 2008 - 2010
DIRECTOR OF STRATEGY
Provided strategic marketing and digital brand management leadership. Worked with clients and internal discipline leads from account management, information architecture, design, engineering, media planning and business development. This includes using market research to fuel integrated marketing programs that utilize interactive, social media, traditional media, PR and events.

- Developed a social media and viral marketing practice
- Led in the development of methodologies and standards for the delivery of account planning and consumer research.

The Old Group, Portland, OR 2007 - 2009
DIRECTOR OF BRAND INNOVATION
Provided overall leadership, vision and direction for clients and company in relationship to digital brand communications. Partner with clients, executive management and department leaders in the development and execution of integrated digital programs. Champion thought leadership in audience research, experience design and analytics.

- Developed a social media marketing practice
- Stewarded company go-to-market strategy with prime focus on digital agency-of-record accounts

Independent Contractor, Portland, OR 2005 - 2007
DIGITAL MARKETING CONSULTANT
Applied consumer insight, cultural trends, technology and creativity to inform and deliver integrated, interactive and social media communication strategies and programs.

- Mapped consumer attitudes and media behaviors to the brand engagement cycle with a focus on the awareness, demand generation, sales and retention stages

Education

B.A. Political Science, Interdisciplinary Honors Program (Magna Cum Laude) – Temple University

The Wharton Management Certificate Program – University of Pennsylvania

HyperLife

http://linkedin.com/in/janedoe11

Figure 2-1: A résumé in the traditional format.

Jane Doe

Digital Marketing Strategist

HOME
1234 SW 56th Pl.
Portland, OR 97223

PHONE
(503)-222-2222

EMAIL
hiremenow11@hotmail.com

LINKEDIN PROFILE
LinkedIn.com/in/janedoe11

BLOG
DigitalGenious.com

TWITTER
@janedoe11

Professional Summary

Seasoned digital marketing strategist and director with deep knowledge of brand stewardship. 17 years experience blending customer insight, creativity, and technology to forge visionary brand experiences.

Experience

Independent Contractor, Portland, OR Present
SOCIAL MEDIA CONSULTANT

Focused on social media marketing for B2C and B2B brands. Expertise covers all facets of social media: strategic planning, content development, influencer relations, program management, analytics/optimization and operations.

Wats It Creative, Portland, OR 2008 - 2010
DIRECTOR OF STRATEGY
- Developed a social media and viral marketing practice
- Led in the development of methodologies and standards for the delivery of account planning and consumer research.

The Old Group, Portland, OR 2007 - 2009
DIRECTOR OF BRAND INNOVATION
- Developed a social media marketing practice
- Stewarded company go-to-market strategy with prime focus on digital agency-of-record accounts

Independent Contractor, Portland, OR 2005 - 2007
DIGITAL MARKETING CONSULTANT
Applied consumer insight, cultural trends, technology and creativity to inform and deliver integrated, interactive and social media communication strategies and programs.
- Mapped consumer attitudes and media behaviors to the brand engagement cycle with a focus on the awareness, demand generation, sales and retention stages

Education

B.A. Political Science, Interdisciplinary Honors Program - Temple University
The Wharton Management Certificate Program - University of Pennsylvania

Skills

Adept at bringing new brands to market, demonstrating thought leadership and enabling cross-functional collaboration. Consummate presentation skills.

Figure 2-2: A résumé in a format that also looks good online.

Writing for an online audience

When you read articles online, do you tend to pass over large blocks of text? If so, then you're like most people who have a hard time sorting through dense paragraphs on a screen. When I first started blogging, I had to completely shift how I wrote to a much briefer format. The truth is that most people *scan* online content most of the time. The same scannability test will be true of your résumé.

Following are a few formatting guidelines to help make your online résumé easier to read:

✔ **Use bulleted points and lists as often as possible.** Bulleted lists are easy to scan, as opposed to paragraphs.

✔ **Shorten your blocks of text.** On the web, using single-sentence paragraphs isn't uncommon (contrary to my daughter's ninth-grade teacher's advice). I tend not to write more than three short sentences per paragraph for online writing.

✔ **Use headers.** Headers are just large, bold headlines used to break content up into sections. Headers can make your text more scannable so it's easier for the reader to follow your train of thought. For example, you may break up a big block of text, like your objectives, into two or three sections: "Who am I," "What can I do for your company," and "Three things that make me different."

✔ **Take advantage of hyperlinking.** The Internet was invented so scientists could link one article to another. If you mention something in your résumé, offer more detail by linking to more information about it. For example, you may link to the corporate website of the companies you worked at or schools you went to. You can also link to your LinkedIn profile or even an online portfolio.

✔ **Put the most important content up top.** The *fold* is the bottom of what's visible onscreen in a web browser before you scroll down. You can read content above the fold without having to scroll down. Some people tend not to scroll down, so content below the fold is often skipped. Prioritize your writing so that important information is what appears first.

✔ **Keep a little white space.** Reading big blocks of text on a computer screen is difficult on the eyes. White spaces can break things up and give your résumé a fresh feel. Refer to Figure 8-2 to see how that résumé uses white space to frame the body of the content.

 To get inspired by some very beautiful résumés, check out the CVParade blog at `http://cvparade.com`.

Focusing on the right keywords

A paper résumé may live only in your portfolio, but an online résumé can live anywhere — and, therefore, be discovered by just about anyone. If you can make your online résumé show up on a recruiter's Google search, then who knows what possibilities may open up for you.

To get your résumé found on Google, you need to practice *search engine optimization,* or SEO, which is the art and science of making websites appear on a search engine's first page. You can practice good SEO skills by sprinkling certain choice *keywords* — nouns that Google reads in a web page to determine the page's relevance to a search query — throughout your résumé.

When job seekers discover keywords, they usually experience an aha moment that helps them grasp the importance of using nouns and incorporating search-friendly keywords in their online résumés.

By using a more popular keyword or job description in your online résumé, you're more likely to be found in an online search. Use your own researched keywords on your online résumé.

Generating a Plain-Text Résumé

Many organizations persist in using outdated applicant-tracking systems (ATS). An ATS electronically handles the whole recruitment process, from sorting large amounts of résumé information to providing a platform for recruiters to leave notes and hand off candidates.

Chances are you'll have to apply online using one of these systems at some point. And rather than just letting you link to your LinkedIn profile, it asks you to upload a plain-text résumé. But when you created your résumé, you probably spent at least 50 percent of the time worrying about how it looks. If you upload it to an ATS with all its text boxes, headlines, and bullets, it would actually look quite bad as plain text.

So even if you have a nice-looking résumé, you also need to have handy a drab, plain-text version. Don't worry — it's super simple to convert.

1. **Open your finished résumé in Word or another word processor.**

2. **Copy all the text in the document.**

3. **Paste the text into a simple text-editing program (Notepad for PC and TextEdit for Mac).** If you're using a Mac, convert the pasted text to plain text.

4. **Spend some time cleaning up any odd formatting, like bullet points that disappeared, odd spacing, or reordering.**

5. **Reapply some formatting you need to make it look good in plain text. Here are some tips:**

   • Make headlines pop by using all caps or enclosing them in a few asterisks.

   • Use five spaces instead of tabs to measure your indent.

   • Use asterisks to replace bullet points.

   • Change columns to a linear flow and take advantage of line breaks and white spaces.

6. **Save the completed file as a plain text document (.txt).**

Using Online Tools to Make Your Résumé Sparkle

Just like résumé writers, who help you with the content of your résumé, certain tools and services can help you make that content look amazing.

✔ **Loft Résumés for the style conscious:** Loft Résumés (http://loftresumes.com) is a marketplace where designers sell their take on what a beautiful résumé should look like. If you check them out, you'll see how one of these works of art would help you stand out from the crowd! Prices typically hover around $99.

✔ **Splash Resumes to make it shiny:** One of the services offered by Splash Resumes (www.splash resumes.com) is a graphic-design service. You send in your nicely written résumé, and you get back a work of art. Use this service to tell your story visually. You can pick a previously designed template or ask for a customized one.

✔ **Rezscore for the hard truth:** Unlike Resunate, Rezscore (http://rezscore.com) doesn't need to compare your résumé to a job description to tell you it sucks. After uploading your document, it generates a surprisingly complete report of what you're doing well and what needs some improvement.

✔ **MyOptimalCareer for a full package:** MyOptimal-Career (https://myoptimalcareer.com) packages its award-winning résumé builder with other career tools, including a cover-letter builder, interview practice module, portfolio module, personal résumé-website builder, and video-résumé tool. The site offers the usual features for your résumé — nice templates, easy to use interface — but it also offers writing help and career guidance. Of the résumé builders I mention in this chapter, MyOptimalCareer probably offers the largest variety of predesigned templates.

✔ **ResumeBear for tracking info:** ResumeBear (http://resumebear.com) offers a document-building tool. But it also offers features to help you track who you send the résumé to, whether they bothered to open it, and if they printed it out. This insider info can help you gauge whether or not you've made progress for that role.

✔ **Jobspice to do your formatting:** When you upload your résumé to Jobspice (http://job spice.com), the tool automatically puts it into a professional-looking format, which could save you hours messing around with headings, columns, and text boxes. In 15 minutes, the tool outputs a nice looking document ideal for e-mailing or printing.

✔ **CVMaker for more formatting:** CVMaker (`http://cvmkr.com`) is a free tool that lets you copy in elements of your résumé. You choose what format you want, and then you can download the finished product. Most of the templates are traditional yet very professional. What's really nice about this service isn't so much the designs but that it exports to plain text.

Embracing the Modern Recommendation

Smart careerists strive to collect agreements from former bosses to vouch for them. Having strong recommendations is essential, and having more of them builds your credibility online. Take advantage of this recommendation blitz by helping your connections write as many high-quality referrals as possible.

Asking for an online referral

When asking a former boss or co-worker for a recommendation, these tips may come in handy:

✔ **Expect a 50 percent response rate.** If you're aiming for three recommendations, send out six requests.

✔ **Follow up your request with a phone call.** Using e-mail or LinkedIn's request system alone can be ineffective.

✔ **Use the online résumé's recommendation system, if it has one.** I hate requests that require me to click around for five minutes just to find the spot where I'm supposed to write. Using the online résumé service's recommendation system makes writing recommendations easier.

✔ **Tell your recommenders how little time it takes to write a recommendation and how much it'll impact your career.** If you put your request into concrete terms, people won't feel like you're asking for a big commitment.

✔ **Make certain the person you choose can offer concrete examples to each of the points you want her to make.** The person you ask should be in a position to draw from experiences with you.

Who to ask for an online recommendation

Having more recommendations is a credibility builder, and it tells LinkedIn's search algorithm that your profile is more important than other profiles, so it puts you on top of a search-results page. Be sure you have a nice mix of the following business relationships as recommenders:

✔ Someone you reported to, such as a supervisor or boss

✔ Someone senior but who you didn't report to

✔ A colleague you worked with in the same group

✔ A colleague parallel in your organization but in a different group

✔ A customer or client who you helped

✔ Someone who worked for you or reported to you

A video résumé may help

Not every recruiter or hiring manager is going to spend time watching video résumés for fun. However, if someone already likes your application and wants to know more about who you are, offering him a video résumé is a great way to demonstrate your personality and communication skills.

The ideal video résumé addresses three key questions:

✔ Who are you?

✔ What motivates you?

✔ Can you do the job?

After you've produced a résumé that addresses each of these points, you're ready to upload it for hiring managers' viewing pleasure.

Chapter 3

Using LinkedIn to Put Your Best Profile Forward

. . . .

In This Chapter

▶ Discovering what makes LinkedIn the highest-leverage job-seeking engine on the planet

▶ Taking a look at the essential components of a good profile

▶ Moving your profile to the head of the pack with applications, recommendations, and more

▶ Figuring out how to grow your LinkedIn network

. . . .

*I*n today's connected job market, your first impression with a potential employer is likely to be an online impression. And LinkedIn — a social network for professionals — is one of the primary locations for an employer to find new talent online. Fortune 500 companies (including many of their executives), small businesses, startups, freelancers, and businesses from hundreds of sectors are on LinkedIn.

Recent studies indicate that tens of millions of people have used social media to find work. Yet recruiters spend just eight seconds on average looking profiles. Nowadays, simply having a profile on LinkedIn isn't good enough — it has to be amazing!

You need to seriously ask yourself this question: Is my LinkedIn profile strong enough, compelling enough, or just simply good enough to make the kind of impression on a hiring manager that can get me an interview?

In this chapter, I reveal the most important elements of creating a LinkedIn profile for job-seeking success, what you need to do to get your profile looking great, and some powerful strategies for growing your network's leverage.

Surveying the Elements of a Winning Profile

An employer looks at three key areas of your LinkedIn profile during the first few seconds of viewing (I show you where these elements can be found in Figure 3-1):

- ✔ Your profile photo
- ✔ Your professional headline
- ✔ Your profile summary

I call these elements the *Big Three,* and they're incredibly important to the effectiveness of your LinkedIn profile.

Profile photo   Professional headline

Linked in.

Joshua Waldman

Author of Job Searching with Social Media For
Dummies | Speaker and Marketing Consultant
Portland, Oregon Area | Internet

Current	**Client Work: Digital Marketing Manager** at **CareerShift, LLC** **CEO and Founder** at **Career Enlightenment LLC (Sole Proprietorship)**
Past	National Account Manager and Social Recruiting Specialist at Avature
	Account Executive at Janrain, Inc.
	Chief Social Media Strategist at Cinta Media Group
	see all ▾
Education	Boston University - School of Management
	Brown University
Recommendations	**36** people have recommended Joshua
Connections	**500+** connections
Websites	My Award Winning Career Blog
	My For Dummies Book

Joshua Waldman's Summary

I am the author of the best selling book, Job Searching with Social Media For Dummies,
which has sold over 10,000 copies in the US and abroad.

I'm frequently quoted by Forbes, Mashable and International Business Times for advice on
using social media to find jobs.

When I'm not writing articles or books, I enjoy presenting to students on finding a job online
and training their career counselors on winning strategies so they always feel ahead of the
curve.

Profile summary

Figure 3-1: A LinkedIn profile featuring the three winning
elements.

Taking a good profile photo

Hiring managers want to know who you are. They want to see whether you have leadership qualities and whether you're friendly and professional. They want to imagine what working with you may be like. All these attributes can be communicated to your advantage with a good profile photo.

Generally speaking, not having a profile photo on LinkedIn can cause you more damage than having a bad one. Many recruiters I talk to say that a blank profile photo lands many qualified candidates into the maybe pile.

A strong LinkedIn profile picture includes the following key elements:

- ✔ **A pleasant smile:** A good photo is warm and welcoming. Show those pearly whites.

- ✔ **Professional attire:** Not every job requires that you wear a suit and tie, but you should dress appropriately. Think about the job you're going for and dress for your first day.

- ✔ **A pleasing background:** Each color and background texture alters the emotional quality of the image. Some people choose green or blue backgrounds, which convey trust and stability. One friend, a financial advisor, stood next to the Merrill Lynch bull to communicate an association with the financial industry.

- ✔ **An interesting angle:** Your profile picture isn't a mug shot, so don't look head on at the camera. Instead, try tilting your head slightly or look at the camera over a shoulder. You want to avoid symmetry around your head.

✔ **A sign of your personality:** A marketing friend of mine used an image of herself playing a Rock Band guitar which helped her land a job in the creative marketing world. Although you don't need a gimmick or prop in your photo, think about what you can do to show who you are and how that image relates to your chosen industry.

✔ **Clear lighting with a close crop:** Because your picture will appear on someone's computer in a very small crop, your face needs to be clearly visible. Be sure you use lighting that highlights your face, and crop so that your face takes up most of the 150-x-150 thumbnail.

Don't crop your face out of your vacation photos. Take your profile picture seriously and find an hour or two to do it right. If you don't have a good camera, see whether your local department store has a family studio where you can get some good, professional shots.

Writing a professional headline

Your professional headline appears just below your name as well as on every communication you send in LinkedIn. It's the first thing someone reads when your profile shows up on a search results page. It defines who you are and what you can do for an organization. That's why LinkedIn doesn't simply call this section *job title,* yet many people make the mistake of stating their role, such as sales executive or VP of Finance.

In your LinkedIn professional headline, you have 120 characters to really communicate your identity — what you do, who you are, and what your level of motivation is. This spot is also your chance to show a hiring manager that you understand the needs of her business. What can you do to help her company?

Because LinkedIn's search algorithm indexes the headline first, be sure to include your most powerful keywords and keyphrases. If you currently have a job, mention it by name in your headline. Employed people sometimes have an easier time finding other jobs. So take advantage of this trend by explicitly calling out your current employer and what you're doing there.

Summarizing what makes you different

The summary section of your profile appears just below your activity at the top of your profile (refer to Figure 3-1). If hiring managers make it as far as your summary, they're essentially asking you to tell them more about you. So here's your chance to make an impression. Whatever you do, don't bore them. Only after reading your summary do hiring managers look at your experience and education.

A good profile summary has these three characteristics:

- ✔ **It's short.** Keep your summary between five and ten lines on the screen, or three to five sentences. When read out loud, your summary shouldn't take more than 30 seconds to read. (And, yes, that means you need to read it out loud with a timer.)

- ✔ **It's concise.** Your summary isn't the place for bulleted lists of your accomplishments, but it should quickly tell viewers more about you.

- ✔ **It's unique.** Avoid jargon, buzzwords, or clichés.

✔ **It's a narrative.** You're welcome to use first person pronouns in your summary. Rather than referring to yourself in the third person, like you would in a résumé, tell your story with *I* and *my*.

Getting Your Profile in Tiptop Shape

Nowadays, first impressions between employers and potential employees are taking place on LinkedIn more and more frequently, which means you need to put the same effort into the way you look online as you do into your physical appearance when you're heading to an interview or meeting.

I want you to have not only a complete profile — one that shows your photo, has at least three recommendations, and includes all the details about your work experience and education — but also an impressive profile that makes you stand out.

If you don't yet have a LinkedIn profile and want basic details about how to set up an account, see the latest edition of Joel Elad's *LinkedIn For Dummies* (John Wiley & Sons, Inc.). Make sure your profile is complete before moving on to the next sections.

Getting the skills to pay the bills

The Skills & Expertise area in LinkedIn is a place for you to highlight what you are really good at and what areas you're currently working on. When you add a Skill to this section, you're quickly helping your reader understand what you can do, not just by adding more descriptive keywords but also by adding another dimension to your profile. Each skill can receive an Endorsement from each person in your network. So skills with more Endorsements quickly reveal what your network thinks you're very good at.

Because LinkedIn has built some uniformity around each skill, you'll see who the top influencers are for the skill, how it's changed over time, related skills, locations where that skill is in higher demand, and much more. This information can help you make better informed decisions about who to connect with, which locations you should focus on, and even what other words people use to describe what you do. Follow these steps to find all this information:

1. **Log in to your LinkedIn account and Head to** http://linkedin.com/skills.

2. **Type in something you're skilled in, like management, ballet, or WordPress.**

   As you type, LinkedIn will make some suggestions based on its own list of skills.

3. **When you see your skill pop up, click on it.**

4. **Check out the page for that skill that comes up. Each page has lots of information to comb through, but pay close attention to Related Skills, Relative Growth, and Relative Size.**

   Use the Relative Size graph found in the upper-right corner to identify smaller niched skills to explore.

5. **Click on See Suggested Skills to learn what LinkedIn suggests for you based on your profile.**

Just like with keywords, there are two strategies to take when choosing skills. You can use skills that have a small, niched use, often called *longtail,* or you can grab more popular skills. Longtail skills make you visible to recruiters who are looking for highly specialized candidates, like for certain programming languages, sales techniques, or other subcategories. When choosing skills, start at the highest level of describing what you do, then narrow down to more specific, longtail keywords.

 If you had to choose between two skills, choose the one with the higher Relative Growth number. On the top right of the page, look for the graph called Relative Growth. This chart tells you which skills are growing, year over year, relative to other related skills. You may find skills with a negative growth rate, which you should avoid.

Endorse this!

Members of your network can vouch for any of your skills by endorsing them. Each skill in your profile can have endorsements, which look like a teeny-tiny icon of the Endorser's face next to your skill on your profile.

In contrast to recommendations (see the next section), endorsements don't require thoughtful responses, complete sentences, or specific details. It's just a quick-click kudos from people who think you're indeed good at that skill.

Over time, you may notice that some skills receive more attention than others. I've been able to validate my personal brand by watching this trend over time. I'm positioned as a speaker on social media topics, and guess what skills are in my top five: speaking and social media. You know your branding is working when the right skills are getting endorsed.

 Anytime you receive endorsements, or when you give them, you have an opportunity to re-engage your network. If someone you haven't been in touch with for a while endorses you, use it as an opportunity to reconnect.

As soon as you enter your skills (see the previous section), you'll start getting endorsed. LinkedIn will pop-up an "Endorse your network" type of box for folks in your network. Then with one click, they can endorse you. However, if you don't want to wait for that to happen, you can take a more proactive approach. Here are some ways you can supercharge your endorsements.

- ✔ **Endorse first:** When you endorse someone, that person receives an e-mail. Often people will recip-rocate. Only endorse people for skills you know they have and you can vouch for.

- ✔ **Ask directly:** If certain people in your network can vouch for some of your skills, feel free to ask them, just like you would ask for a recommendation.

- ✔ **Join an Endorsement Group:** Although this prac-tice goes against the intention of endorsements, you can join a group and get endorsed by total strangers, just to get your numbers up.

Requesting really good recommendations

Recommendations in LinkedIn allow you to send or receive professional references and display them on your profile in a trustworthy way. You need at least three recommendations to have a complete LinkedIn profile.

The recommendations section is the one part of your profile that you don't have full control over because you have to rely on other people to write these recommendations for you (which makes them more reliable). I've noticed that LinkedIn's search algorithm ranks profiles with more recommendations higher than others. If you want to be found, I highly encourage you to take your recommendations seriously.

As a general rule, you want to have recommendations equal to about 5 to 10 percent of your network size. So if my network has 280 people in it, I may strive for 28 recommendations, but 14 is good enough. Of course, only about half the people you ask for a recommendation will respond. So if you need three recommendations, send out six requests. If you want 10, send out 20.

 The trick with requesting recommendations on LinkedIn is to always personalize your request message. LinkedIn drops some standard language into the request form, but you need to tailor this note for each person you're asking. By suggesting a few bullet points for them to cover in their recommendation, you make it easier for them to think of something to say, or remind them of a specific event where you leaped over buildings in a single bound.

Updating your status

LinkedIn's status update feature allows you to post a short message to share with your network (first- and second-degree contacts only — in other words, the people you're directly connected to and the people they're directly connected to). The functionality of status updates on LinkedIn is very similar to that of

Facebook and Twitter. In fact, when you link your Twitter account to your LinkedIn profile, your LinkedIn updates can be sent to your Twitter feed as well.

Think of the status update as a quick way of telling people in your network what you're up to. You can find status updates just below your professional headline at the very top of your profile (see Figure 3-2). Other people see your update on their home page and may even have it included in a weekly e-mail from LinkedIn.

Figure 3-2: Status updates are a good way to communicate within your network.

The more recruiters you have in your network, the more chances you'll have of getting discovered. Consider doing whatever it takes to get as many recruiters in your network as possible. Go to an Advanced People search using the keyword Recruiter and add as many as you can.

Adding the people you already know

Now that your profile is something to be proud of, be certain that everyone you know has received an opportunity to connect with you on LinkedIn. This is the fastest way to grow your network.

✔ **People you know from e-mail:** Click on the Add Connections icon at the top-right corner of your LinkedIn profile. Here, you can import e-mail addresses from your e-mail clients and invite your contacts to connect on LinkedIn.

✔ **People you know from work or school:** LinkedIn makes predictions of people you may know based on what you filled out in your Experience section and Education section (so be sure these sections are filled out accurately first!). From your LinkedIn Home page, click on People You May Know. You'll see a long list of possible candidates. From there, you can choose a company or a school through which you know these people. Click through these and connect with anyone who looks familiar.

 Use LinkedIn's Alumni tool to quickly find others from your graduating year to connect with. Log in to your LinkedIn account and go to http://linkedin.com/alumni to find these advanced search features. To find people you might know, set the graduating year to match your own.

Growing your network en masse

The following statement may sound silly, but here goes: The more connections you have on your LinkedIn profile, the more likely hiring managers are to trust you. They see your large network as a sign that others validate you and that you're worth getting to know.

When growing your LinkedIn network, you have to decide whether you're a Cat or a LION. *Cats* are more conservative networkers who add only people they know, and in some cases, they must have had at least a 15-minute conversation with them. *LinkedIn Open Networkers,* or LIONs, are more liberal networkers and can have networks as large as 15,000 connections or more.

The magic number of LinkedIn connections is 143 — and not just because numbers that end in three are lucky! If you have fewer than 143 connections, chances are you're not going to have second- or third-degree connections in any of the companies you want to work for. If you have more than 143 connections, your next goal should be to get 500 or more connections.

Becoming a LION

If you find yourself with fewer than 143 connections (or fewer than your target number like 500+), I suggest you take a more liberal approach to growing your network. Consider becoming a LION for a short time. At the very least, consider finding and inviting a handful of LIONs to join your network. Their large networks serve to increase your second- and third-degree connections substantially. So even if you don't want to add tons of strangers to your network, at least the few LIONs you do add can give you some substantial benefit.

Following are a few ways to promote yourself as a LION:

- ✔ Put "LION" next to your last name in your profile.

- ✔ Enter your e-mail address in your profile summary and say, "Invites welcome."

- ✔ Join several open networking groups, such as Lion500, TopLinked, or Open Networker. To find more, just do a group search for "open networking."

- ✔ Go to the Members tab at the top of any open networking group. In the search area, search for members in your area of interest.

Whenever your network reaches the size and depth you're comfortable with, simply stop being an open networker.

 One disadvantage to being a LION for too long is that your network is filled with strangers. This means you're not in a strong position to ask for introductions to target companies. I highly suggest you use your LION status sparingly to just help you over the first few humps of getting to your target number of 143 or 500 connections.

Being a cat

If you have a comfortably large network (any number larger than 143) and don't require the gung-ho networking of a LION, then you can afford to be a bit more catlike in picking who you connect with. (*Cat* doesn't stand for anything but is just a more careful way of growing your LinkedIn network.)

Here are some steps you can take to strategically (and tactfully) grow your network:

1. **While logged in to LinkedIn, click on the Advanced link at the top of your LinkedIn profile to access the Advanced People Search page.**

2. **Type in one of your keywords in the Keywords field or simply use your industry, such as advertising or accounting.**

3. **Click on the Search button.**

4. **Deselect 1st degree and group in the relationship settings, leaving behind the 2nd and 3rd degree filter**

Your search results list new people in your strategic area who may be open to connecting with you. Take your time and look at each profile. If you've joined any of the open networking groups, you may already be members of the same group and can invite them without using an e-mail address.

Generally, if people include their e-mail address in their profile, it means they're open to networking with you.

Joining groups to expand your brand

A LinkedIn *group* is a collection of professionals connected around a common theme. A group's main function is to facilitate discussions and networking within a trusted environment. The two kinds of LinkedIn Groups are *open groups,* where membership isn't mandatory to participate, and *closed groups,* where you need to join to read discussions and network. Some closed groups may accept your request to join automatically. Others require an administrator to approve your membership based on some criteria.

Paying for LinkedIn or going free?

Many people commonly wonder whether they should pay for LinkedIn. LinkedIn has certainly made it easy for job seekers to do so by offering a discounted membership level. Additionally, I pay for LinkedIn and use the advanced features almost every day. However, my answer isn't so cut and dry. Many people find enormous benefit to the free version. So here's my advice: Use the free version until you're limited by some restricted feature. You may need more Direct Messages, Invitations, or advanced search filters. If you're bumping up against this wall, then consider jumping into a paid account for the duration of your job search. You can always cancel and go back to the free version after you land a job, when you don't need to use LinkedIn so much.

Chapter 4

Uncovering the Hidden Job Market with Twitter

- -

In This Chapter

▶ Setting up a polished Twitter profile

▶ Using Twitter to grow your professional network

- -

*T*witter offers a forum for short messaging (all messages are 140 characters or fewer) among any of its members, from CEOs to mailroom clerks. This hierarchical flattening and instant communication make Twitter the most useful — albeit the most misunderstood — tool for a job seeker.

In this chapter, I demystify Twitter for you and explain why adding it to your job search doubles your effectiveness as a networker. I also cover important etiquette topics so you can rest easy knowing you look good to everyone in the Twitterverse.

 Your online reputation is as important to your job search as dressing well for an interview. Having an active Twitter account means your name will rank in Google almost right away. And as employers discover more about you

through your Twitter account, you can rein-
force your personal brand to support your
candidacy for a job.

How Twitter Can Help You Find a Job

Hiring agents, internal HR staffers, headhunters, large
human-resources firms, and private recruiting professionals use Twitter to actively fill open positions. Why?
Because posting job openings on Twitter is not only
free but also effective as a way to advertise positions to
a smaller pool of engaged professionals.

When a recruiter posts a job, he usually uses a hashtag
to indicate that the tweet is about a job posting, for
example, *#job, #career,* or *#hiring,* followed by a short
description and a link to the position's online page.
The link typically takes you to the job posting on the
recruiter's website, where you can apply directly.

Companies and recruiters don't typically use Twitter to
fill jobs beyond simply announcing openings; however,
I've heard of some creative companies asking candidates to apply for a job using Twitter directly. Applying
for a job in just 140 characters is a lot harder than you
think!

As a job seeker, you can use Twitter to find work in
essentially two ways. First, Twitter allows you to create
instant relationships within target organizations.
Second, you can monitor job opportunities posted on
your Twitter timeline like a real-time job board.

Setting up Your Twitter Profile for Job Searching

After you decide to give Twitter a try for your job search, the easiest part is setting up your profile (unlike LinkedIn, where the hardest part is setting up the profile, but I help you figure all that out in Chapter 3).

When you create a profile on Twitter, you first focus on picking a username and writing your *bio* — a brief self-description that appears on your Twitter home page.

Choosing your name and username

Your name appears only in your Twitter profile, but your *username* (what you go by on Twitter; also called a *handle*) is attached to every tweet. Your username is also the domain name for your profile.

When picking a username, remember that its length eats away at your 140-character message. The longer your username is, the less space you have for your messages.

If your name is long, consider abbreviating it, or use a keyword or description of your profession in a short and memorable way.

To set your name and username for the first time, simply head to www.twitter.com, click on the Sign Up button on the right-hand side of the screen, and fill in the required fields. If you already have a Twitter account and want to change your username, head to the top-right portion of the page, click on your current username, and then click on Settings. From there, you can make any desired adjustments to your username.

Changing your username often isn't wise because you want people to instantly recognize you, and your username helps accomplish that. Pick a username you can live with for a while; it's going to become a strong part of your personal brand.

Your name and username form a *title tag* on your Twitter profile page. This title tag appears in the Internet browser's window. Google uses title tags as part of its search algorithm, which is a good reason to use your full name combined with your best keyword when choosing your Twitter name and username. Because Google indexes Twitter several times an hour, your chances of ranking on Google's first page for your name and keywords are quite high.

Writing your 160-character bio

Google uses your bio to index your Twitter account, so those 160 characters may be the first splash of information someone gets about you. For that reason, I recommend thinking of your Twitter bio as a sales pitch. People decide whether or not to follow you based on what they read in your bio. And because Twitter users are bombarded with thousands of followers and tweets every time they log in, your bio needs to grab their attention, make them curious, and cut through all the clutter.

A good way to describe yourself on Twitter is to imagine that you're at a networking event at a bowling alley and responding to someone's request to "Tell me about yourself." In Twitter, you can add a bit more personal color to your image, as illustrated in the following examples:

Future focused finance executive. I know the weather & wear a rain jacket for changes in economic climate. Looking to fly a company above the storm clouds. (155 characters)

IT Project Director specializing in web-based reporting. If it ain't broke, I'll make it even better. I want your systems working elegantly. (140 characters)

Recent grad not looking forward to moving back in with parents. Love communications and creative problem solving. Amateur film critic with published reviews. (157 characters)

Knowing What (And What Not) to Share

Google displays your last two tweets in search results for your name, and people often read these tweets before deciding to follow you. So what you do and don't tweet about (and how frequently you tweet) is extremely important.

You're using Twitter to get a job. You don't have to be stuck-up, hidden away, or always on topic; however, keep in mind that a hiring manager may see your tweets, in which case getting too casual is a mistake. Be personal sometimes, but not all the time.

Deciding what to tweet

Typically, the hardest step in getting started with Twitter is figuring out what on earth to say. Don't worry. If you can carry on a conversation, you can tweet. Posting links to articles and retweeting good posts from others are great ways to get started, but you'll want to get more personal after a while. The following list gives you an idea of the kinds of personal details and experiences that may be worth sharing:

- ✓ **A quote:** Quotes are some of the most treasured tweets out there. Start collecting short quips to share on Twitter. If you hear a great one-liner in a movie or read something profound in a book, tweet it. Make sure you use the hashtag #*quote* to let your followers know you're being pithy.

- ✓ **A question:** After you have more followers, consider asking them questions. Questioning your network is a great way to build relationships.

- ✓ **Something special you do:** If you do something special or unusual, share it. Ask yourself, "Does sharing this allow someone else a chance to feel closer to me?"

- ✓ **Something you see:** If you see a killer sunset, snap a photo and share it with your followers. They may appreciate it, too. Use apps like Pheed or Instagram on your phone to do this easily.

- ✓ **An insight:** If you have an opinion, a pet peeve, or a flash of insight about a topic, why not let your followers know?

- ✓ **A recommendation:** Did you meet someone remarkable who helped you? Share your experience on Twitter and help promote your benefactor.

- ✓ **A direct communication:** If you find someone you want to talk to, why not start a conversation? Use @[username] in your tweet to alert the other person. As long as your post doesn't look like spam, chances are you'll get a reply.

Discerning what not to tweet

Never share personal information that can be used
against you or that can be used to impersonate you,
such as the following:

- ✔ Your birth date
- ✔ Your phone number
- ✔ Your address
- ✔ Your mother's maiden name
- ✔ Details about your children
- ✔ When you're going on vacation or leaving your home
- ✔ Potentially damaging images or information about yourself

Seeking a Job, Twitter-Style

Finding and following your target companies on Twitter
can be a fun way of driving your job search. However,
companies you may never have heard of are posting
jobs and recruiting on Twitter as well. Setting up a *listening station,* a list of current tweets based on keywords
you can view, helps you monitor and track all the important job-seeking activities going on around you.

Every major metropolitan city has a human-resource
industry wherein recruiters build a list of possible candidates to place into possible jobs. More and more,
these recruiters are turning to Twitter to post jobs
and recruit talent. Follow these steps to find your local
recruiters so you can monitor real-time job postings:

1. **Go to any Twitter user directory and type the following into the search box: "recruiter, *[your city]*" or "executive search, *[your city]*."**

   I prefer `http://www.followerwonk.com`.

2. **Follow the firms who are active on Twitter.**

   Check their past few tweets to see whether or not they post regularly.

3. **Add your finds to a Recruiters list so you can follow their posts easily.**

 The Local Buzz Network (`http://localbuzz network.com`) aggregates jobs and news from over 250 cities around the United States. Each city has a Twitter feed and e-mail newsletter to distribute local information. For example, if you live in Newark, New Jersey, you would follow @newark_buzz to read about local jobs and news. Use the hashtag *#jobs* to just see job-related posts.

Many cities have people who are so passionate about Twitter's job-networking ability that they maintain a Twitter account that aggregates job postings in your area. These Twitter accounts are great resources for uncovering the hidden job market. Here's how to find them:

1. **Visit your preferred Twitter user directory and type "*[your city]* jobs" into the search box.**

2. **Find the Twitter accounts that are streams of job listings.**

   Often, these streams are broken down by industry, such as healthcare jobs or internships.

3. **Follow these streams and add them to a list called Local Jobs.**

Another way to uncover the hidden job market on Twitter is to perform persistent searches for words and hashtags that contain the words *jobs, careers,* and so forth. As jobs are posted in your area, you'll be able to see them and apply for them in real-time. Just follow these steps:

1. **Create a new column for searching a keyword in your Twitter-management software.**

   HootSuite and TweetDeck are two common types of Twitter-management software.

2. **Type in a job-related hashtag, such as *#jobs, #careers,* or *#employment.***

3. **Further refine your search by using variations of your location.** For New York City, also include NY and NYC.

TweetMyJobs (www.tweetmyjobs.com) is a great Twitter job-searching platform available. As a job seeker, you need to engage in three primary activities on TweetMyJobs:

✔ **Subscribe to a job channel.** A *job channel* is simply a Twitter feed that's specific to your location and industry.

✔ **Upload your résumé and then tweet a link to download your résumé to TweetMyJobs's exclusive @TweetAResume account.** Doing so sends a link to your public-facing profile to thousands of followers.

✔ **Create a social profile.** Companies that post jobs through TweetMyJobs can view social profiles, so creating your own profile is like getting added to a company's database of viable candidates.

Understanding hashtags

Hashtags, which are preceded by the # symbol in Twitter, are subject markers. They're used to create continuity within the chaos of the thousands of tweets being posted every second. Recruiters post jobs by using several different hashtags. Here are some hashtags worth searching for in Twitter:

#career	#jobpostings
#careers	#jobs
#employment	#jobsearch
#hire	#jobseeker
#hireme	#jobseekers
#hiring	#laidoff
#job	#recruiters
#jobhunt	#recruiting
#jobhunting	#work
#jobinterview	

Chapter 5

Using Facebook as a Job Hunter

*F*acebook has defined a generation, changed general perceptions regarding privacy, and inspired an army of entrepreneurs. Job seekers who don't take ownership of their Facebook accounts may pay the highest price.

Why is Facebook so essential? Most jobs come from referrals, and most referrals come from friends and family. Guess which social network has the highest concentration of friends and family.

Also, you can use Facebook to find out more about a company. Just by "liking" a company's Facebook page, you can find links to the company's blogs and websites, as well as information about benefits, culture, and other important HR information.

This chapter shows how to take advantage of your Facebook profile to aid in a job search.

Editing Your Profile for Hiring Managers' Eyes

With Facebook, you can communicate your personal brand, or unique message, through strategic parts of your profile. And you're able to take advantage of your trusted network to spread the news about what you're looking for and the value you bring to the table. After all, most jobs come from people you know through your network.

When you first set up your Facebook account, I'm sure you didn't have professional networking in mind, so now's the time to revisit your profile and make some changes.

Your Facebook profile can be made visible to people who haven't joined your network yet. If you spend time and fill it in, then nosy hiring managers and recruiters can learn more about you. Your profile info also helps Facebook find new people to suggest you add to your network. The more accurate you are in your profile, the more accurate Facebook's suggestions are for who else you can connect with. Making sure your profile is filled out is worth the extra five or ten minutes.

> ✔ **Your profile photo:** In Facebook, your profile
>   photo is attached to every communication you
>   send and is considered basic information in your

privacy settings. The reason is that Facebook is first and foremost a visual platform.

✔ **Your cover photo:** The larger banner behind your profile photo is called your cover photo. Pick images from your life that mean something to you, like a nice picture of your family at a wedding, or a beautiful day at the beach where the sunset just took your breath away.

✔ **Your About Me section:** Your About Me section should serve a very similar function as your LinkedIn profile summary, in that it communicates who you are professionally and what makes you unique. The text you enter in this can be set to appear publicly and may be the only prose a hiring manager conducting some preliminary screening may read about you on Facebook.

If you're actively seeking work, I recommend pasting a copy of your value statement in the About Me section of your profile.

✔ **Work and education:** Be sure your work and education history information matches that of your LinkedIn profile. Hiring managers are looking for inconsistencies (after all, some people lie on their résumés), so if they see that you're consistent with your résumé in several places, they're more likely to believe you.

✔ **Favorite quotations:** Sharing who inspires you and what your favorite quotes are can be powerful ways of differentiating yourself.

Practicing Good Timeline Etiquette

Facebook is more about posts than it is about profiles.
Your most important message is your last post. Literally.
Eye tracking studies show that most eyeballs spend the
most time reading the last post on someone's timeline.
The Facebook timeline is your venue for communicating
with your network and letting people know who you are
and what you're looking for. The timeline is an amazing
platform for expressing yourself, but you need to use it
wisely.

- ✔ **Don't be desperate.** Avoid posts like, "Help! I need
  a job. Can you pass my résumé on?" You don't
  want to come across as desperate.

- ✔ **Start conversations.** Unless you're a celebrity,
  posting about yourself all the time won't get you
  many comments. You may have to start conversations from time to time. Ask questions, post an
  article and share your opinion of it, or bring up
  something from current events.

- ✔ **Share industry-related content.** At least once a
  week, post something related to your industry
  and set the privacy to Public

- ✔ **Ask for introductions:** Nothing's wrong with
  asking your network for a little help sometimes.
  Because the power of your network is in who the
  people in it know, the best thing you can do to
  help yourself is to ask for introductions.

Be specific when asking for a referral. You inevitably get much better results if you can say the name of the company and the exact role of the person you want to meet.

Finding People to Network with Using Graph Search

Graph Search is a way to explore Facebook's network of information about people. Graph Search can be found at the very top of your Facebook Profile. By using search phrases instead of keywords, you can discover all sorts of people in and outside of your current network.

Pitching Your Value (Statement)

A great way to let people know who you are and what you're all about is to post your value statement on your timeline every once in a while. An added bonus of posting your value statement on your timeline is that you can ask for direct feedback about it regarding what works and what doesn't. As long as you don't overdo it — meaning don't post your value statement every day — your friends will give you feedback and help you make your value statement better.

Journaling Your Job-Search Journey

Use Facebook as a platform to share your job-seeking progress with friends and family. Let them know what steps you took that week to find work. Share interesting insights about yourself or about job seeking in general. Celebrate your successes, like having finished your résumé or getting a callback from a target hiring manager.

Using Promoted Posts to Make Sure Your Message Is Seen

Not everyone in your network reads every post you publish. With Facebook's filters and friends list, there really is no way to guarantee that your message will get read. But you can get pretty darn close by using promoted posts.

Promoted posts are posts that have a guaranteed audience. Prices can go up to $10 depending on the type of post and how large the audience would be. You can promote anything in your post. After you post it, click on Promote.

Promotion is a great way to get your value statement out to a larger audience. If people haven't visited your profile or commented or chatted with you in over two weeks, chances are they aren't hearing much from you on Facebook. Use promoted Posts to rekindle cooling relationships.

Math & Science

Algebra I For Dummies, 2nd Edition
978-0-470-55964-2

Anatomy and Physiology For Dummies, 2nd Edition
978-0-470-92326-9

Astronomy For Dummies, 3rd Edition
978-1-118-37697-3

Biology For Dummies, 2nd Edition
978-0-470-59875-7

Chemistry For Dummies, 2nd Edition
978-1-1180-0730-3

Pre-Algebra Essentials For Dummies
978-0-470-61838-7

Microsoft Office

Excel 2013 For Dummies
978-1-118-51012-4

Office 2013 All-in-One For Dummies
978-1-118-51636-2

PowerPoint 2013 For Dummies
978-1-118-50253-2

Word 2013 For Dummies
978-1-118-49123-2

Music

Blues Harmonica For Dummies
978-1-118-25269-7

Guitar For Dummies, 3rd Edition
978-1-118-11554-1

iPod & iTunes For Dummies, 10th Edition
978-1-118-50864-0

Programming

Android Application Development For Dummies, 2nd Edition
978-1-118-38710-8

iOS 6 Application Development For Dummies
978-1-118-50880-0

Java For Dummies, 5th Edition
978-0-470-37173-2

Religion & Inspiration

The Bible For Dummies
978-0-7645-5296-0

Buddhism For Dummies, 2nd Edition
978-1-118-02379-2

Catholicism For Dummies, 2nd Edition
978-1-118-07778-8

Self-Help & Relationships

Bipolar Disorder For Dummies, 2nd Edition
978-1-118-33882-7

Meditation For Dummies, 3rd Edition
978-1-118-29144-3

Seniors

Computers For Seniors For Dummies, 3rd Edition
978-1-118-11553-4

iPad For Seniors For Dummies, 5th Edition
978-1-118-49708-1

Social Security For Dummies
978-1-118-20573-0

Smartphones & Tablets

Android Phones For Dummies
978-1-118-16952-0

Kindle Fire HD For Dummies
978-1-118-42223-6

NOOK HD For Dummies, Portable Edition
978-1-118-39498-4

Surface For Dummies
978-1-118-49634-3

Test Prep

ACT For Dummies, 5th Edition
978-1-118-01259-8

ASVAB For Dummies, 3rd Edition
978-0-470-63760-9

GRE For Dummies, 7th Edition
978-0-470-88921-3

Officer Candidate Tests, For Dummies
978-0-470-59876-4

Physician's Assistant Exam For Dummies
978-1-118-11556-5

Series 7 Exam For Dummies
978-0-470-09932-2

Windows 8

Windows 8 For Dummies
978-1-118-13461-0

Windows 8 For Dummies, Book + DVD Bundle
978-1-118-27167-4

Windows 8 All-in-One For Dummies
978-1-118-11920-4

e Available in print and e-book formats.